by

Al Jaffee

A SIGNET BOOK

NEW AMERICAN LIBRARY

TIMES MIRROR

NAL BOOKS ARE ALSO AVAILABLE AT DISCOUNTS IN BULK
QUANTITY FOR INDUSTRIAL OR SALES-PROMOTIONAL USE.
FOR DETAILS, WRITE TO PREMIUM MARKETING DIVISION,
NEW AMERICAN LIBRARY, INC., 1633 BROADWAY,
NEW YORK, NEW YORK 10019.

PUBLISHER'S NOTE
The *Introduction* to this book is a fanciful parody and not
intended to be read as factual with regard to the cartoonists
parodied, their methodology, or their work product.

∅

SIGNET TRADEMARK REG. U.S. PAT. OFF. AND FOREIGN COUNTRIES
REGISTERED TRADEMARK—MARCA REGISTRADA
HECHO EN CHICAGO, U.S.A.

SIGNET, SIGNET CLASSICS, MENTOR, PLUME and
MERIDIAN BOOKS
are published by The New American Library, Inc.,
1633 Broadway, New York, New York 10019

First Signet Printing, January, 1980

1 2 3 4 5 6 7 8 9

PRINTED IN THE UNITED STATES OF AMERICA

INTRODUCTION
How Famous Cartoonists Work

Every single day all over the world millions of people enjoy cartoons in books, magazines, and newspapers. Although the cartoon is one of the oldest art forms, few people actually know how cartoonists work. Just as each person's fingerprints are exclusively his own, so are cartoonists' methods of working. Two of the earliest examples are shown below.

Primitive man making comic drawing

Comic man making primitive drawing

Cartoons were a smashing success right from the start. Through pestilence and plague, famine and war, nuclear leak and TV commercial, cartoons have brought a measure of sanity and comic relief to us all. But how do these brilliant little masterpieces come into being? What implements are used to create these images of joy and laughter?

Let's find out.

POOPY by Bud Saggydrawers

Bud's wonderful characters are whipped out in the amazing manner shown here. When asked how he likes working this way, he always answers, with a popeyed grin, "It's a real snap when you know how!"

RODNEY RODENT
by Walt Dipsy

Here we see how one of the world's best-loved cartoonists works. It all started as a practical joke when Walt's friend Donald ducked behind a bar and slipped him a mickey. Walt immediately started acting goofy—dipping his finger in an ink bottle and shmearing it all over. The walls, which were snow-white a minute before, were now covered with dozens of marvelous cartoons. Thus, Walt's famous finger-shmear method of cartooning was born.

THROWING UP FARTHER
by Geo. McMinus

George's most unusual drawing technique involved taking a big gulp of ink and then spewing it out onto a drawing surface. This astonishing technique, inspired by fellow cartoonist Mack Miller, eventually resulted in the creation of two of the world's most famous cartoon characters—Jinks and Naggy.

EXTRAORDINARY PERSON
by Seagull and Shystar

Using an ordinary housepainting brush, this extraordinary team created the fantastically popular cartoon feature known the world over. It was truly a super feat by supermen.

DICKY TRICKY by Chest Cold

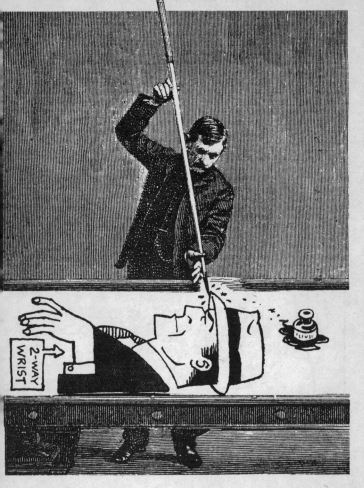

One of the most remarkable cartoon techniques is the one employed here, a cue stick dipped in India ink. During fifty years of cartooning, this great storyteller has sparkled plenty of times and never once has he wound up behind the eight ball.

HORROR THE HAGARD by Dik Clown

Dik's cartoons are direct and to the point. And so is the spear that he loves to draw them with. Dik also does another brilliant feature known as "Howdy and Louse," which, just for diversion, he draws with an old mace.

DUMMI by Irwin Handsome

Put a mason's trowel in Irwin's hand and he creates sheer magic. He also likes to work dressed in the way he was created—in sheer nothing.

PISTACHIO NUTS by Sparky Snoops

Actually, what Sparky always wanted to be was a great musician. Then, when he found out that most musicians work for peanuts, he decided to create a great comic strip instead. But just to keep his hand in music, he developed the famous ink siphon hornblowing technique shown here.

DUNEBUGGY by G. B. Turnblue

This extraordinary cartoonist has a hair-raising experience every time he sits down to work. We tip our wigs to this talented fellow. His Pulitzer Prize surely places him head and shoulders above the crowd.

COCKROACH BAILEY
by Mort Whopper

Mort's feather-light touch tickles an army of readers all over the world. In his private life, Mort loves to join all kinds of organizations. He also enjoys working while wearing club uniforms, one of which is shown here. It is of the International Order of the Beetle.

ANATHEMA GRUMP by Bill Hoist

Bill loves the outdoors, rain or shine. In fact, he's often too confused to tell whether it's raining or shining. But when this great cartoonist has to lock horns with an art problem, an old stick dipped in ink soon solves everything.

ECCH AND YECCH
by Hoohah Schneider

Hoohah's amazing umbrella technique startled even his professional colleagues. "Any bimbo can eke out a meek living drawing with a pen," says the high-flying Hoohah. "But an umbrella offers something more. Especially if you live in an area where it rains three hundred and sixty-four days a year like I do."

SEEDYMAN by Stan Lip

"Stan has a nose for cartooning," his teachers used to say. So when Stan grew up, he took them literally and used his nose to create a host of famous cartoon characters. "It's all a marvel to me," humbly says Stan of his great success.

NEVILLE THE NAUGHTY by Hank Ketchup

Facing a blank sheet of drawing paper every day is a real menace to Hank. But it is a great challenge, too, which he meets with rapier, wit, and ink.

BLEACHEDHEAD by Young Chick

This talented artist grew up in a remote area of the Midwest. Since no drawing instruments were available there, young Young had to make do with what he could find around the farm. He soon discovered that a large stalk of wheat worked just fine. With it he went on to create the world-beloved Bleachedhead and her husband Dogwood.

A.D. by Johnny Mopp

Johnny's method of working, though misleadingly prehistoric in appearance, is sublimely sophisticated. Using old cigar butts, Johnny rubs them into any available surface, and like a true wizard makes magical images appear.

NOSY by Ernie Bushwacker

In school, Ernie's teachers made him stand in the corner so often he began to see the world backward. Naturally, when he took up art the same thing happened. To this day he draws his lovable little "Nosy" character with a pen held over his shoulder while standing with his back to the easel.

A faithful-hound episode
that should be thrown to the dogs

MORE

③

(4)

MORE

(6)

You want to know how I went BATTY?
READING THIS BOOK, **THAT'S** HOW!

Oh, I beg your pardon. You see, I was painting a stripe down the road when . . .
DO NOT CROSS WHITE LINE
MEN WORKING

35

A travel story
that goes absolutely nowhere

A story about beach sand without a grain of merit

①

(4)

TOWN GRADE SCHOOL

Cartoon Folio Number Three

57

A thinking story
that's mindless and dull

3

(6)

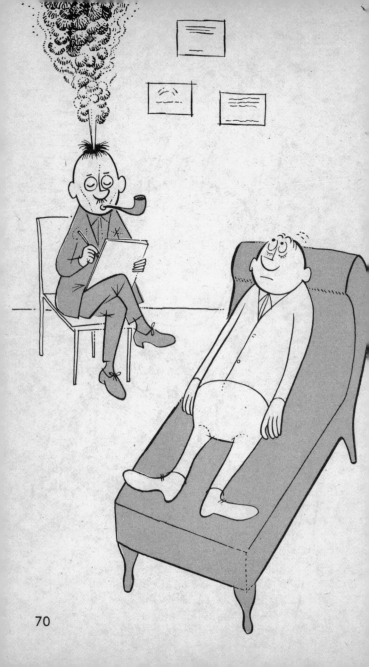

RENT
A
CAR CO.

WE
RENT
ALL
MAKES
AND
MODELS

TOMATO

A welcome mat story
that turns people away

MORE 75

HON. HOMER E.
SENATOR FROM

They've certainly captured **your** thirty-six years on Capitol Hill, Homer.

78

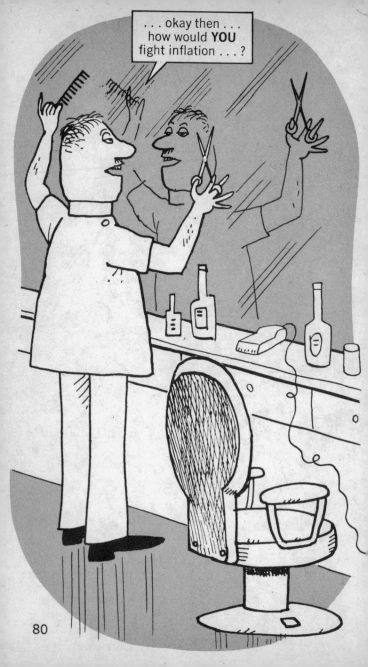

②

3

4

Cartoon Folio Number Six

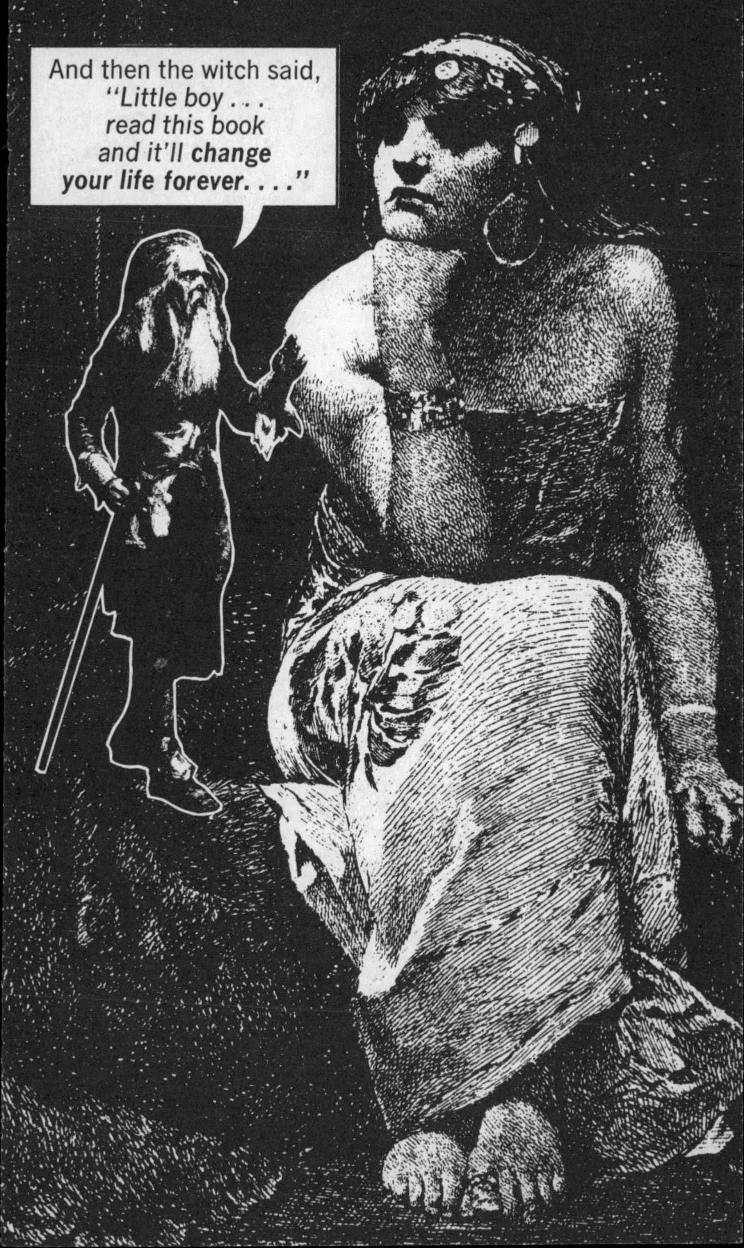

NUCLEAR
PLANT
#2

89

An office experience
you can file and forget

MORE

3

MORE

6

A suggestion-box sequence that we can fill with complaints

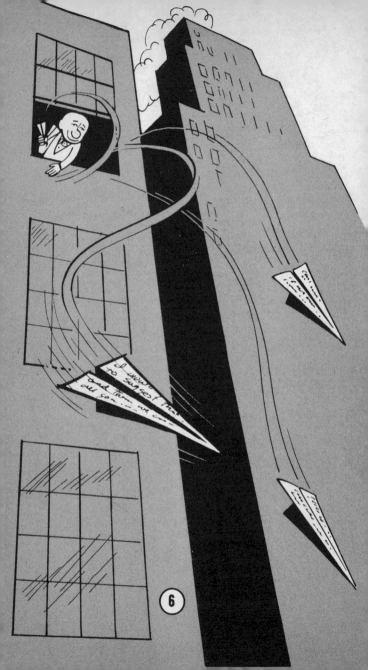

FAULTLESS
CONSTRUCTION
COMPANY

A masquerade tale
that's thinly disguised bunk

MORE

①

Cartoon Folio Number Nine

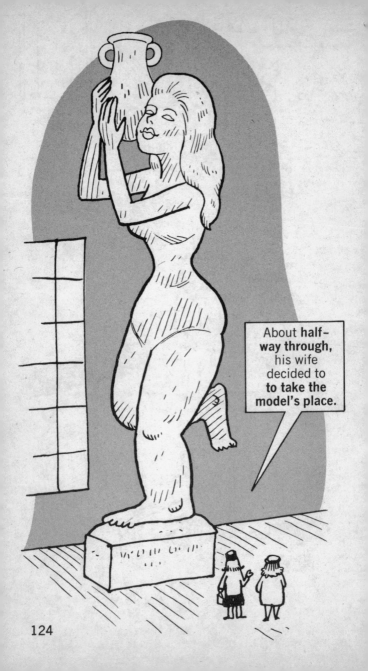

About **half-way through,** his wife decided **to take the model's place.**

An exercise story
that's awful flabby

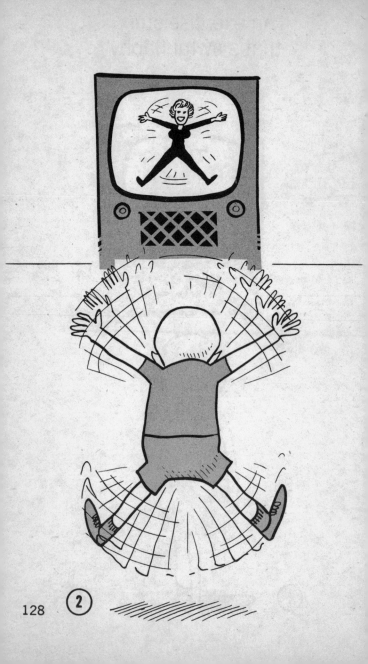

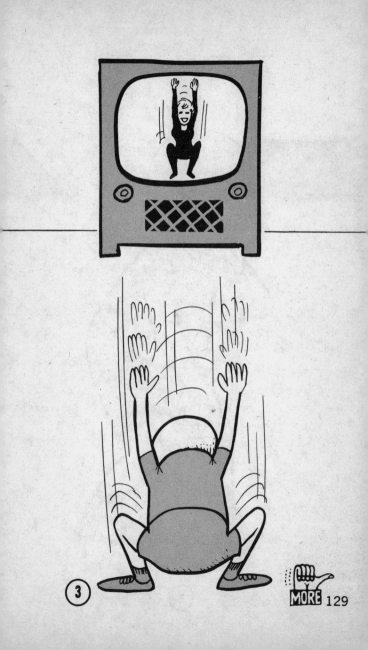

④

137

A marching-band saga that should be drummed out of existence

① ——

(4)

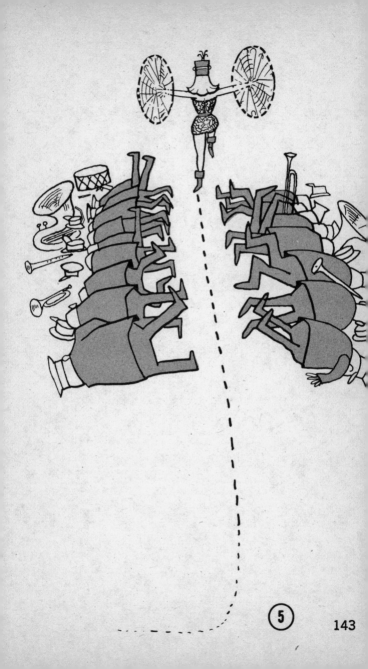

146

147

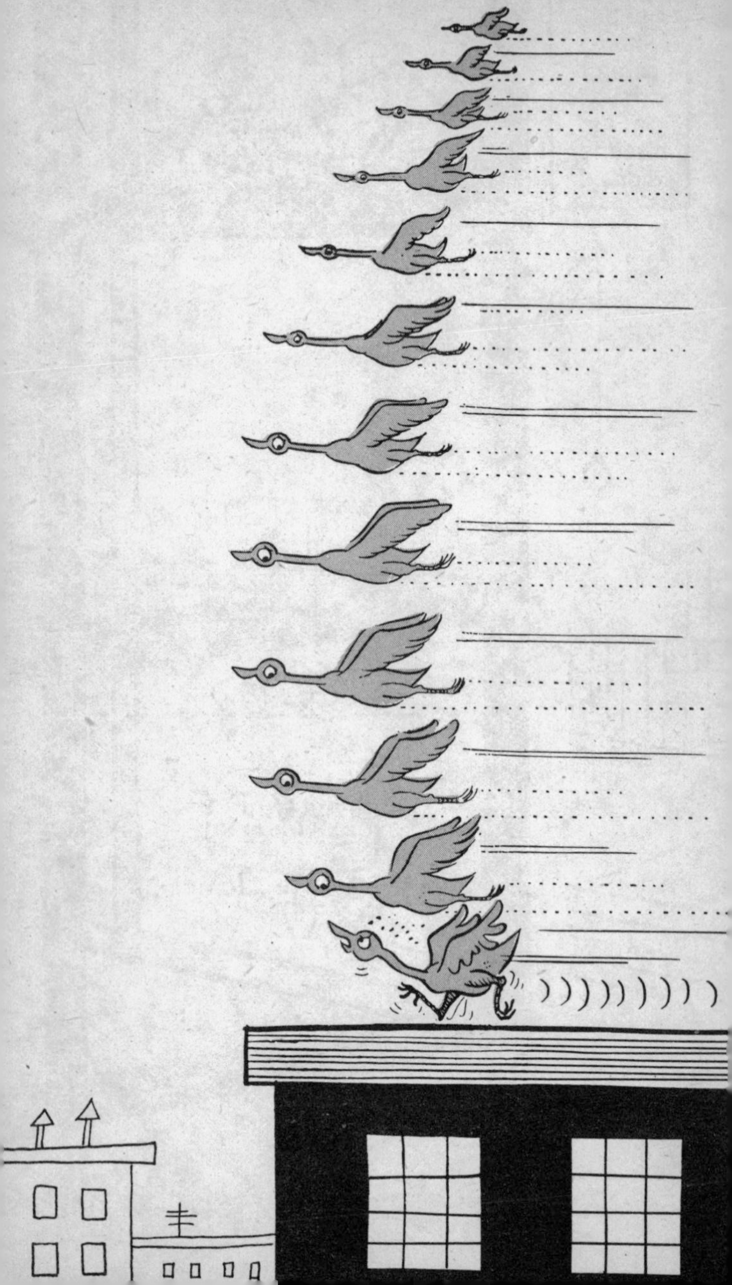

An underground-sewer adventure that hits a new low

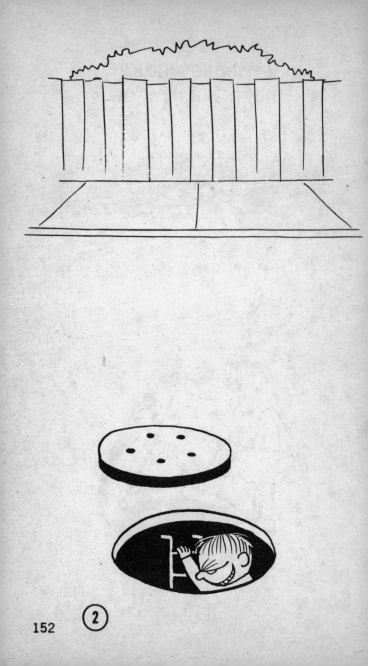

②

MORE

Cartoon Folio Number Twelve

158

161

A story about a flood that's a complete washout

① MORE 163

②

③

168

TODAY'S
ENGINEERING
LECTURE

DAM
CONSTRUCTION

169

A dogcatcher sequence that's like something the cat dragged in

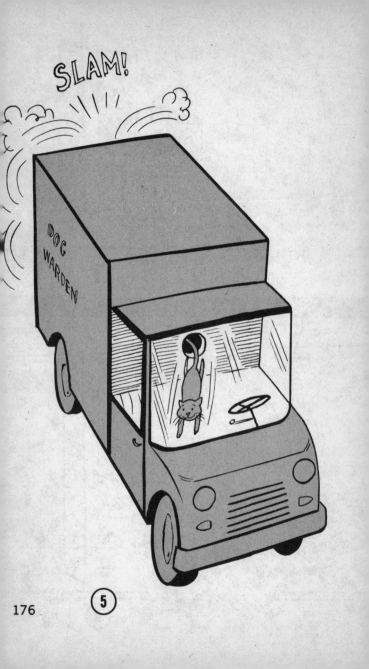

A TV experience
with a very low rating

②

MORE

③

Until a few moments ago
this guy was a *happy-go-lucky*
cheerful fellow.
Then he *turned to the next page*
and *collapsed in grief.*
So *please*—if you *don't want your day ruined,*
go away quietly
without looking at the next (yicch!) page.

HURRY, HURRY, HURRY!
BUY THESE BOOKS!
68
Only 12, 256,671 copies of these treasured . . .
classics left in stock.

☐ Al Jaffee Gags . . . . (#Y6856—$1.25)

☐ Al Jaffee Gags Again . . . . (#Y6552—$1.25)

☐ Al Jaffee Blows His Mind . . . . (#Y6759—$1.25)

☐ More Mad's Snappy
Answers to Stupid Questions
by Al Jaffee . . . . (#Y6740—$1.25)

☐ The Mad Book of Magic
by Al Jaffee . . . . (#Y6743—$1.25)

☐ Al Jaffee's Next Book . . . . . . (#Y7625—$1.25)

☐ Rotten Rhymes and
Other Crimes by Nick Meglin
Illustrated by Al Jaffee . . . . . . (#Y7891—$1.25)

☐ Al Jaffee Bombs Again . . . . . . (#Y7979—$1.25)

☐ Al Jaffee Draws A Crowd . . . . . (#Y8226—$1.25)

☐ Al Jaffee Sinks to a New Low . . (#W9009—$1.50)

☐ The Ghoulish Book of Weird
Records by Al Jaffee . . . . . . (#W8614—$1.50)*

☐ Al Jaffee Meets His End . . . . . (#W8858—$1.50)*

* Price slightly higher in Canada